# Bridging the GAPS

## A Journey to the Center of Your Self

A Workbook & Guide

*for Women*

to Heal the Wounds of Life &
Live True to Your Sacred Essence

Debra Graugnard, M.Div.

Joyfully Living Publications

A Small Town in Texas

# SPREAD YOUR WINGS, LADYBUG!

The Ladybug symbolizes a time "in which our wishes begin to be fulfilled. Higher goals and new heights are now possible. Worries begin to dissipate. New happiness comes about. This insect also cautions not to try too hard or go too fast to fulfill our dreams. Let things flow at their natural pace. In the due course of time, our wishes will all come true. Alternatively she could be signaling that you can leave your worries behind and that new happiness is on its way. This species of beetle signals you to not be scared to live your own truth.

**"Protect your truth and know that it is yours to honor."**

Ladybug symbolism from  www.Spirit-Animals.com/ladybug.
Above photo from Adobe Stock Photo © constantincornel #104945102
Cover photo from Adobe Stock Photo © Laura Pashkevich #123548394

NOTE TO THE READER:  If you have a physical, mental, emotional or spiritual condition, or if are a trauma survivor, make sure you put your safety measures in place.  You might want to seek support from a professional therapist of your choosing and not traverse this healing journey alone.  Approach your process with self-love, self-care and gentle loving kindness.

DISCLAIMER:  This book is designed to provide information and inspiration to readers.  This book is not intended to diagnose, prescribe or cure any conditions or ailments.  This book is distributed with the understanding that the publisher and the individual authors are not engaged in the rendering of psychological, legal, accounting or other professional advice.

Published by Joyfully Living Publications
Copyright © 2019 Debra Graugnard

www.JoyfullyLivingPublications.com
www.JoyfullyLivingWellness.com

ISBN: 978-1-7331046-0-9

# Dedication

This book is dedicated to all who travel this journey called life seeking to heal the wounds and live true to your sacred self.

May your heart be held in love and compassion.

May you find healing for your body, mind, heart and soul.

May you find peace and safety inside your skin.

May you develop trust in yourself.

May you realize your own beauty.

May you know the depths of your Divinity.


On behalf of all the contributors to this project:

We see you.

We hear you.

We feel you.

*We believe in you.*

"What you seek is seeking You."

~ Jalal ad-Din Rumi

# Workbook Contents

"You are a volume in the divine book.
A mirror to the power
that created the universe.
Whatever you want, ask it of yourself.
Whatever you are looking for
can only be found inside yourself."

~ Jalal ad-Din Rumi

# Who this Workbook Is For

This workbook is for women seeking to heal from the wounds of life and live from the deepest truths of their sacred essence. This workbook guides you through a powerfully effective healing journey to the center of your Self.

No matter what your challenges have been, the pitfalls, griefs, traumas and wounds of life separate you from yourself. In the pursuit of love and survival, you develop beliefs, coping strategies, defense mechanisms and survival tactics to keep yourself safe in a world that can feel pretty distant from the love you were born to know. Before you realize it, you've amassed so many barriers of protection that you can't find yourself. But rest assured, the real you is still in there. This is the You that guided you here.

The exercises in this workbook will help you uncover and rediscover the truths of who you are - the truths that got buried as you traveled through life. The process laid out in this book will guide you to embody and live into your inner Sacred Essence so you can live a life that is true to your heart and soul.

The journey you will travel as you embrace these exercises is a powerful one. To drop into the innermost secrets of your divine self, you must be willing to let go of the outer meanings you've ascribed to the events of your life. As you let go of the attachments that may have once provided you a sense of safety and connection, you can view your life events through a wide lens that encompasses the purpose of your soul's pathway through this trip to planet earth.

This book is based on spiritual principles. The principles are not specific to any religion, but it helps if you have a belief in a power higher than yourself, one that is all-encompassing with a wisdom that extends beyond the 3D material realm that is based in our present time and space reality.

Several times throughout the workbook, I suggest calling on your Highest Power, guides and angels for support. They are part of a whole support team helping you at any given time. We have free will, so in most cases they will not intervene until we ask for help. They are not bound by the perceptions accessible through our physical bodies and five senses. They can see things we cannot. So why not ask? They are waiting.

# Who this Workbook Is For

This book makes a great guide for a group experience. I highly recommend gathering a group of like-hearted women who are interested in healing, self-empowerment and spiritual transformation to go through these chapters together. Perhaps meet weekly and go through one chapter each week, allowing time for exercises and discussion. Between meetings you can focus on the journaling and allow the processes from the previous week to integrate. Be sure to watch for signs that your intentions are coming into manifestation. You'll find more about this with each chapter.

You can check our website for virtual gatherings. BridgingTheGAPSWorkbook.com.

If you've experienced severe traumas that have left you with gaps in your memory, flashbacks, recurring dissociation or other retraumatizing patterns, please take extra care of yourself. You may want to seek assistance from a professional therapist to support you on this journey.

In any case, if this description calls to you, Welcome! This is your book. Make it your own. Follow your heart, gut, intuition, guidance. Feel free to tweak a bit here and there. Do what you need to do to make the processes work for you.

You're in for a powerful journey of self-discovery, healing and transformation!

Thank you for embarking on this journey.
Blessings,
Debra

"There is a journey of healing ahead of you
when you are ready for it -
to reconnect, to rebuild the bridge
back to your sacredness."

~ Lisa Hare, from While We Were Silent

This workbook is for me because...

_____

_____

_____

_____

_____

_____

_____

"We're all just walking each other home."

~ Ram Dass

"When you do things from your soul,
you feel a river moving in you,
a joy."

~ Jalal ad-Din Rumi

# How to Use this Workbook

Your healing journey is unique and personal, only for you. You are the guide on your journey. You have the authority to decide what you want to receive from this workbook. You can determine the pace that feels right for you and how deep you want to go with each exercise. You can decide who you would like to travel with on your journey. That said, you may find it valuable to do this process with a group.

This workbook is intended to help you reflect on what is important and true for you, to identify and shed some of the beliefs that are not yours, to determine what you truly need, to uncover your deepest knowings and to honor who you are. This is a pathway to Bridge the GAPS between the life you are living and the life you are truly meant to live; to Bridge the GAPS between who you are being now and who you were born to be.

The chapters in this workbook are intended to be taken in order, as each chapter builds on the previous ones. It is designed to complete roughly one chapter per week, your Weekly Focus. You may find it helpful to read each section a couple of times before doing the exercises.

I recommend coming back to this book every day to journal, using days in between weekly focus exercises for reviewing and reflecting upon intentions, priorities and your commitment to yourself, and writing your affirmations. There are prompts for writing and re-writing your responses, which will help you solidify their presence in your consciousness.

Re-reading and rewriting your intentions and affirmations Bridges the GAPS between head and heart. It establishes energy pathways from your heart through your arm to your hand to the page, from the page to your eyes to your consciousness and back to your heart.

With each section, you will find exercises for Bridging the GAPS between where you are now and where you want to be. This process calls on you to recall your Gratitudes, Affirmations and Positive Signs (GAPS). These are designed to help you bring your thoughts and desires from energy form into manifestation - from concept into realization - from thoughts and wishes into real experiences in your life.

# How to Use this Workbook

You will also find Creativity & Doodles pages throughout the book. This is for expressing yourself outside the lines. Use these pages as you wish. Creative artwork can help you release fear, tension and stuck energies from your body.

Finally, at the end of each chapter are journal pages where you can share Reflections and Ruminations that are revealed for you as you traverse these exercises.

Throughout the workbook, I mention calling on your guides for support and guidance. Are you familiar with this concept? You have an incredible support team helping you on your earth journey. They are cheering you on. They include your Source or Highest Power (insert the words that fit with your beliefs), angels, prophets, guides, helpers, healers, ancestors and more. They are available and waiting to be called upon. We humans have been given free will, so they have to wait for us to ask. And when we do ask, they can move into action to help.

You are also welcome to reach out to our community for support. Know that you are not alone. Many have walked this path, and many are walking it with you. Someone here can relate to what you are going through, and they can be there for you and with you. You do not have to travel alone.

You are welcome to join our online community. Find this information and other support resources at BridgingTheGapsWorkbook.com.

Blessings for you on your journey.
Thank you!
Debra

~ The 5 R's ~

1. Review Your Intentions daily - preferably each morning and evening. You'll set this in Chapter 1.

2. Make it Real - experience it, embody it and live it.

3. Repeat - write and recite your intentions and Affirmations until they become second nature. Put them where you will see them often.

4. Reflect - challenge yourself to feel the process in your body and notice the subtle shifts. Journal your Gratitudes, Reflections & Ruminations.

5. Reinforce what you receive - write the Positive Signs of success and evidence of your intentions coming to fruition.

## On Creativity & Doodles...

*"When you are fearful, you tend to stay tensed up.
When you start doing the larger creative movements,
you open up the body and you start releasing things.
You feel things you haven't felt before."*

*~ Dalzenia Sams, Artist for Peace, from While We Were Silent*

"Just because you can't drink all that falls
doesn't mean you give up taking sips of rainwater."

~ Jalal ad-Din Rumi

# 1: Setting Your Intention

Have you been divinely guided in your life? Perhaps a voice comes in to help you through a challenge or you sense a tap on the shoulder guiding you to your next step. It is no accident you've ended up here. Something has guided you here, and it speaks to you through your intuition and your heart.

When you sense a calling from inside, a spark has been lit in your heart to guide you toward a gift that awaits for your soul. The gift is already there, waiting for you to acknowledge it and say yes.

Take a minute now. Relax into your space. Take a deep breath into your heart space. Feel the spark inside. What is it that you want? Breathe into your heart and allow your breath to fan the flame of yearning, the inspiration inside you.

Energy flows where attention goes. Bring your awareness to your heart energy center and listen. It might help to put your hands over your heart. Take your time... Breathe... Feel... Trust yourself... The yearning is what calls you home.

Our first step is to listen for what has called you here and to make a note of it. No need to overthink it. You don't have to get the perfect all-encompassing answer right away. Begin with a sip. You don't have to catch every drop of rainwater. You can tweak as you move through the exercises.

NOTE: If you need help connecting with your heart, visit BridgingTheGapsWorkbook.com for support materials.

*The calling inside me is*  _____

_____

_____

_____

_____

_____

_____

# 1: Setting Your Intention

Now that you know what called you here, let's set an intention. This will help you to have an idea of where you're going. The destination might change. On the healing journey, no doubt it will at least take a detour here and there. But you can set a direction for each leg of your trip. This step of setting an intention will help you determine where you want to go as you're starting on this pathway.

*To intend* literally means *to move toward*. Setting an intention is making a declaration to move toward something. The previous exercise guided you to listen for what called you here. It guided you to acknowledge a gift that awaits for your soul, a gift that is already present waiting for you to say yes to it.

What is that calling guiding you to move toward? Say yes to that movement by stating an intention. Your intention does not need to be perfect or all-encompassing. It can be simple, and it may change over time.

If you don't know, you may want to start with something like, "I intend I have clarity on where I am and what is important for me." You can reassess and tweak your intention at any time. Your intention gives you a starting point and initial direction.

Remember, energy flows where attention goes, so state your intention in the positive - what you are moving toward, not what you are moving away from.

For example, if you are being called to greater self-acceptance and self-love, a positive intention would be, "I intend that I love and accept myself," instead of "I intend that I stop judging and criticizing myself."

Review your calling from the previous page. What is it calling you to move toward? State your intention below...

*I intend that* _____

_____

_____

_____

# Bridging the GAPS

When you take a step to acknowledge and move toward the call of your heart and soul, the Universe conspires to support you to receive it.

Watch for signs of support. You might notice old doors closing. New doors opening. Burdens lifting. People showing up in your life with helpful connections. You feel gratitude for things you took for granted before. Even the signs of nature appear differently.

Notice and acknowledge even the subtle signs. Energy flows where attention goes. Bridge the GAPS by focusing on Gratitudes, Affirmations and Positive Signs. This will increase the flow of energy and open the space for more support of your intentions to flow into your life. It will align and open you to receive your intentions into your life in a concrete way.

If you haven't noticed anything yet, ask for help from your guides. There is much support available to you. Be specific and relevant, and follow the flow to bridge the GAPS.

## GRATITUDES

*Today I am grateful for* _____

_____

_____

_____

_____

_____

_____

_____

# My courageous heart guides me through my healing process with gentle loving kindness.

Write & Recite the above affirmation
and/or add your own based on your intention:

_____

_____

_____

_____

_____

_____

_____

_____

_____

_____

_____

_____

# POSITIVE SIGNS

_Signs that the Universe supports my intentions are_ _____

_____

_____

_____

_____

_____

_____

_____

_____

_____

"You have survived the challenges and traumas of life.
No matter how the situations or incidents appear,
you have the courage to move forward because
you have made it through this far.
You were strong enough to survive.
You are already courageous,
and you can and will make it
through the healing process."

~ Rev. Dr. Anthousa Helena, from While We Were Silent

# Reflections & Ruminations

# Reflections & Ruminations

"Allow your sense of your highest guidance to send out
an invitation to all the exiled parts of your being...
All the relative parts of yourself are welcome
to join the circle of unity."

~ Neil Douglas-Klotz

# 2: Committing to Yourself

In Chapter 1, you touched into what calls you to make a change, and then you set a personal intention for yourself. Congratulations! Great work!

Now we're about ready to dive in. Before we do, use the following pages to write a letter to yourself to support you in realizing your intention. It can be to yourself as you are right now and/or to your inner child who is accompanying you on this journey.

The letter is from you - your highest self that witnesses all the parts of you. This is the part of you that seeks healing and wholeness to unify all the parts of you to live in harmony with your deepest inner truth.

Sometimes we feel we have been abandoned by those we most depended on to care for us. In an attempt to disconnect from the pain, we disconnect from ourselves. In a sense, we abandon ourselves, but this is out of need and a will to survive. This is normal, a natural part of the life journey that every human gets to experience. Please don't beat yourself up. If you have already been hard on yourself, this might be a good time for forgiveness.

It's never too late to return to ourselves and to commit to be present for ourselves now. If it feels like too much to do in one step, you can commit to be open to returning to yourself, to be open to allowing for the unfolding that will come as your healing progresses.

From where you are now, what are the words you need to hear to support you in your intention? What commitment do you need from your highest self? What promise can you make to yourself to see this through - for both of you, for all of you?

Again, this is your journey. Make it work for you.

Date: _____

Dear _____,

_I commit to you_ _____

_____

_____

_____

_____

_____

_____

_____

_____

_____

_____

_____

_____

_____

_____

_____

_____

_____

Your Signature -->          _____

_____

# Bridging the GAPS

When you take a step to acknowledge and move toward the call of your heart and soul, the Universe conspires to support you to receive it.

Watch for signs of support.  You might notice old doors closing.  New doors opening.  Burdens lifting.  People showing up in your life with helpful connections.  You feel gratitude for things you took for granted before.  Even the signs of nature appear differently.

Notice and acknowledge even the subtle signs.  Energy flows where attention goes.  Bridge the GAPS by focusing on Gratitudes, Affirmations and Positive Signs.  This will increase the flow of energy and open the space for more support of your intentions to flow into your life.  It will align and open you to receive your intentions into your life in a concrete way.

If you haven't noticed anything yet, ask for help from your guides.  There is much support available to you.  Be specific and relevant, and follow the flow to bridge the GAPS.

## GRATITUDES

*Today I am grateful for* _____

_____

_____

_____

_____

_____

_____

_____

_____

# I believe
# in ME.

Write & Recite the above affirmation
and/or add your own based on your intention:

_____

_____

_____

_____

_____

_____

_____

_____

_____

_____

_____

_____

# POSITIVE SIGNS

_Signs that the Universe supports my intentions are_ _____

_____

_____

_____

_____

_____

_____

_____

_____

_____


"So key, so essential,
is that we actually decide
we are going to choose ourselves."

~ Licia Berry, from While We Were Silent

# Reflections & Ruminations

# Reflections & Ruminations

"Out beyond ideas
of right-doing and wrong-doing,
there is a field.
I'll meet you there."

~ Jalal ad-Din Rumi

# 3: Finding Your Starting Point

Who does your intention call on you to be?  For years I looked for examples of women who embodied traits of the person I wanted to be.  I was looking for someone to model what I wanted to find in myself.  In my case, it was the sacred feminine self.  I wondered, "What is that really?"

The truth is, the sacred self is an experience that you discover within yourself, just like your inner truths, your purpose, your connection with Spirit and the spirit within you.  The intention you've set likely asks something of you.  What does it call forth from within you?

Even though it's an inside job, it helps to look outward to discern what is important to you - what resonates with what you know inside?  What does your inner knowing find attractive and what does it find repelling?  Your reactions to your outer environment give you important information about your inner values.

There are many role models that our media broadcasts before us - including social media.  Some traits are positive and some not, yet all of them leave some imprint in the psyche.  Whether it's a Hollywood figure or musician, a politician, thought leader, historical figure or religious figure, or someone close to you, their personas and how the masses respond to them leave an impact.

Which ones are important to you?  Which have left an impact on you?  Is the impact positive or not positive or both?

| Role Models | Positive | Not Positive |
|---|---|---|
|  |  |  |
|  |  |  |
|  |  |  |
|  |  |  |
|  |  |  |
|  |  |  |
|  |  |  |

Use the chart below to sort out the desirable and not-so-desirable traits based on the Role Models you listed.  These may also be general characterizations.

| Desirable Traits | Not-so-Desirable Traits |
|---|---|
|  |  |

Now place a STAR (*) next to each of the items in the left column (Desirable Traits) you want to develop within yourself.  Next, place a STAR (*) next to each of the items in the right column (Not-so-Desirable) that you would like to clear from your psyche, personal habits, or beliefs.

# 3: Finding Your Starting Point

Now from the starred items on the previous page, select your top 1-2 Priorities and make a note about why you selected them and what you hope for.

Your priorities allow you to hone in on the personal work you can do to bring about the manifestation of your intentions.

Priority #1: _____

*This is important to me because*_____

_____

_____

_____

_____

On a scale of 1-5, with 1 being "I am looking for a way to get there" and 5 being "I'm there 100%," answer the following:

Where I want to be (A): _____ Where I am (B): _____ Gap: (A - B) _____

Priority #2: _____

*This is important to me because*_____

_____

_____

_____

_____

On a scale of 1-5:
Where I want to be (A): _____ Where I am (B): _____ Gap: (A - B) _____

# Creativity & Doodles

# Bridging the GAPS

When you take a step to acknowledge and move toward the call of your heart and soul, the Universe conspires to support you to receive it.

Watch for signs of support. You might notice old doors closing. New doors opening. Burdens lifting. People showing up in your life with helpful connections. You feel gratitude for things you took for granted before. Even the signs of nature appear differently.

Notice and acknowledge even the subtle signs. Energy flows where attention goes. Bridge the GAPS by focusing on Gratitudes, Affirmations and Positive Signs. This will increase the flow of energy and open the space for more support of your intentions to flow into your life. It will align and open you to receive your intentions into your life in a concrete way.

If you haven't noticed anything yet, ask for help from your guides. There is much support available to you. Be specific and relevant, and follow the flow to bridge the GAPS.

## GRATITUDES

_Today I am grateful for_ _____

_____

_____

_____

_____

_____

_____

_____

_____

# I acknowledge and accept
# ALL OF ME
# with Love and Gratitude.

Write & Recite the above affirmation
and/or add your own based on your intention:

_____

_____

_____

_____

_____

_____

_____

_____

_____

_____

_____

_____

# POSITIVE SIGNS

_Signs that the Universe supports my intentions are_ _____

_____

_____

_____

_____

_____

_____

_____

_____

_____

_____

"Most importantly, know that you are a being of light.
No matter what has ever happened to you in your life,
the light inside you stays intact.
The events of your life do not define you.
They merely form a pathway upon which you may indeed lose yourself.
But then you find yourself,
this time with the eyes of your heart and soul
that recognize the depths of your divinity. "

~ Debra Graugnard, from While We Were Silent

# Reflections & Ruminations

# Reflections & Ruminations

"You may not control all the events
that happened to you,
but you can decide
not to be reduced by them."

~ Maya Angelou

# 4: Making Space for the Truth to Emerge

When you set intentions to improve your inner living conditions, some of the old dusty cobwebs will naturally be cleared out - and no doubt some of them will resist giving up their quarters. Perhaps they've been there for a long time keeping watch over your windows and doorways doing their best to keep you safe.

The cobwebs are the old lies we hold onto about ourselves and our lives. Some are yours and some never have been, but you've been hanging onto them as a way to make sense of your life events or maybe to protect others you have cared about.

They may reveal themselves in subtle ways. They show up as belief patterns that don't make sense any more, old habits that are not in your best interest, coping strategies, defense mechanisms and survival tactics that are not healthy for you.

The old ideas don't always let go so easily. They resist change. Their resistance can undermine your best efforts toward making a new life for yourself. This is a natural part of the healing journey.

It helps to acknowledge some of the patterns you'd like to change in advance, as best you can. Of course you won't know all of them, but you likely have an idea of some patterns that are still hanging around despite your best efforts to wish them away.

*The inner voice that says you can't... or you don't deserve... The recurring relationship that keeps you from doing what you want to do for you... The voice that says this isn't going to work, just go back to sleep...*

These are all forms of resistance. On the next page, you're asked to create a list. As you progress through the chapters, when you feel resistance coming up, you can refer to the list and see if the resistance is a sign that something is trying to let go. If so, you can thank it for wanting to protect you and let it know you are choosing to release it. Then welcome in what you are making space for - with Gratitude. If needed, call on your guides for help.

## 4: Making Space for the Truth to Emerge

First, remind yourself of your intention and priorities:

*I intend that*_____

_____

_____

_____

_____

_____

My Priorities are:

#1: _____

#2: _____

*"Why we feel the way we feel*
*is the result of a symphony and harmony*
*of our own molecules of emotion*
*that affect every aspect of our physiology,*
*producing blissful good health or miserable disease."*

*~ Candace Pert, PhD*

# 4: Making Space for the Truth to Emerge

In the chart below, in the left-hand column list some of the thoughts, beliefs, habits, emotions, stories and relationships that you would like to let go of.  In the right-hand column list what you are making space for when the item on the left is released or transformed.

| I'm letting go of... | I'm making space for... |
| --- | --- |
|  |  |

# 4: Making Space for the Truth to Emerge

To reiterate:  As you progress through the chapters in this workbook, you will likely experience some of your old patterns trying to let go while being met with resistance. Sometimes it feels unpleasant or difficult.

Resistance is a natural part of the process, and it goes along with what you sign up for when you embark on a path of healing, personal development or spiritual transformation.

Resistance is actually a sign that the Universe is supporting your intentions.  Hint: You can even list it under Positive Signs.

When you encounter the challenging times, return to the list you just made.  Is there something on that list that is trying to let go?  If so, look to the column at the right. What are you making space for?

Take a minute for gratitude.  Thank the energy that is resisting release for its service to you.  It is likely hanging on because it has provided some form of safety for you.  Let it know that you are wanting to try another way.  If you need it again, you can always call it back in.  Meanwhile, invite it to take a break.

Then celebrate what you are making space for and welcome it in.

Having this list to return to in difficult times can make the difference between abandoning the process and your commitment to yourself or persevering to the completion of your process to realize true transformation and the life of your dreams.

*Resistance is a sign that something wants to change.*
*It is a sign that the Universe is supporting your intentions.*

When you're in a FOG of resistance, remember
FOG = Freaking Opportunity for Growth

# Bridging the GAPS

When you take a step to acknowledge and move toward the call of your heart and soul, the Universe conspires to support you to receive it.

Watch for signs of support. You might notice old doors closing. New doors opening. Burdens lifting. People showing up in your life with helpful connections. You feel gratitude for things you took for granted before. Even the signs of nature appear differently.

Notice and acknowledge even the subtle signs. Energy flows where attention goes. Bridge the GAPS by focusing on Gratitudes, Affirmations and Positive Signs. This will increase the flow of energy and open the space for more support of your intentions to flow into your life. It will align and open you to receive your intentions into your life in a concrete way.

If you haven't noticed anything yet, ask for help from your guides. There is much support available to you. Be specific and relevant, and follow the flow to bridge the GAPS.

## GRATITUDES

_Today I am grateful for_ _____

_____

_____

_____

_____

_____

_____

_____

_____

# I am a being of Light
# on a path of discovery
# to know my True Self.

Write & Recite the above affirmation
and/or add your own based on your intention:

_____

_____

_____

_____

_____

_____

_____

_____

_____

_____

_____

_____

# POSITIVE SIGNS

*Signs that the Universe supports my intentions are*

_____

_____

_____

_____

_____

_____

_____

_____

_____

_____

*"If you're hurting inside, first reach out to yourself,
look in the mirror and forgive yourself.
Understand that when you heal that space,
you open it up for something much more to rush in."*

*~ Carla Foster, from While We Were Silent interview*

# Reflections & Ruminations

# Reflections & Ruminations

"Empty your cup so that it may be filled; become devoid to gain totality."

~ Bruce Lee

# 5: Whose Is This?

Now we're ready to do a bit of housecleaning. We begin the clean up with clearing out what is not yours to carry. Many of the emotions, beliefs and memories we carry with us are not ours. Many people offer advice, cautions and "wisdom" about our lives, mostly in an effort to protect us. Others impress opinions on us which are based on what they believe about themselves. On some level, we take them in as truths. This is natural. However, these are not *your* truths.

If you have felt judged or been violated or abused, the persons who hurt you likely carried a host of their own emotions and beliefs, including shame, anger, and even guilt. Some of that may have been transferred to you.

Possibly, you are carrying other people's pain and secrets in order to protect them and yourself. You also carry memories from ancestors of events that you have never consciously known. You're not alone. This is human nature.

In any case, other people's beliefs are colored by their own lenses through which they see the world. Their lenses are infused with their experiences and their hurts. We are now choosing to clean our lenses, beginning with clearing out other people's energies.

If someone else's windshield is in front of your eyes and their windshield is clouded with smeared bugs, you don't have to clean it for them. You can return that windshield back to its original owner or give it to your guides to do what is necessary according to a higher wisdom.

In this step, we will offer a ritual. I will describe it for you, and you are welcome to make it your own so it works for you.

## What you will need:

1. Loose scraps of paper.
2. Something to write with.
3. A quiet private space.
4. A candle, bowl of water, paper shredder, or trash bag. Be safe.
5. A supportive friend, if you choose.

## THE RITUAL:

1. Call on your Source of Highest Intelligence, your guides, the angels of healing and all forces of the Universe that conspire to support your healing and wholeness.

2. Trust in their loving support that surrounds you. Feel it if you can. Take a minute to rest into it and breathe it in.

3. Ask them directly for help with releasing what is not yours to carry. They know what that is. Trust in their wisdom.

4. If you know of some of the energies you carry that belong to other people, write them on loose scraps of paper. You can refer to the list you created in Chapter 4 under "I'm letting go of..." Write each on a separate piece of paper.

5. On a final piece of paper, write the following: "Anything remaining that is ready to be released."

6. Take each paper one at a time. Read it, and recite the following:

   "With the help of Source/God/Spirit (your word for your Highest Power),
   my guides, angels of healing and all
   forces of the Universe that support my healing and wholeness,
   I release you from my body, mind, heart and soul,
   and allow you to be returned to your rightful place."

7. Place the paper into a safe candle, a bowl of water, a paper shredder, or tear it up and put it in the trash. As you release the paper, feel the hooks release from you, energies dissipate, freedom set in. Breathe. Let it all go. Receive. Let it land.

8. Continue repeating steps 6 & 7 for each piece of paper ending with the paper created in Step 5, "Anything remaining..." Trust in the wisdom and power of the Universe to support you and facilitate your healing.

9. Now give thanks directly to Source, your guides, the angels and all forces of the Universe that support your healing and wholeness. Breathe and let it all go. Receive. Let it land.

## RECLAIM YOUR ENERGIES:

Next, you are going to reclaim all the parts of yourself that you have given away to others or abandoned outside of yourself.

Before you call all the parts of you home, sit in a still centered space, enjoying the spaciousness and freedom you gained from the cleansing ritual you just completed.

Imagine yourself surrounded by a protective filter that completely encompasses you like a shield. This shield will filter out any unwanted energies or particles from the parts of your self that you are calling back in.

Now call to all the parts of your self and invite them to return home to you. As they pass through the filter, they are cleansed of any energies that are not yours or any unwanted debris.

Welcome them into your core. Feel them taking up their rightful place within you. Feel them strengthening your core. Feel yourself becoming stronger and more complete. You are whole.

Again give thanks directly to Source, your guides, the angels and all forces of the Universe that support your healing and wholeness. Breathe and let it all go. Recieve. Let it land.

Now, move to the next page and recite the Light Prayer.

# THE LIGHT PRAYER

*Call Directly to your Highest Power and ask…*

Please fill me with Your Light.
Please fill my heart with Your Light.
Please fill every cell of my body with Your Light.
Please fill my conscious and subconscious mind with Your Light.
Please fill all of my expansive soul with Your Light.
Please fill and illuminate my core spirit with Your Light.
Please fill and infuse my highest intellect with Your Light.

Please place Your Light in front of me.
Please place Your Light behind me.
Please place Your Light to my left side.
Please place Your Light to my right side.
Please place Your Light beneath me.
Please place Your Light above me.
Please place Your Light within me.

Please make me to be All Light.
Please reinforce my core with Your Strength.
Please envelop me in Your Protection.

Thank You.

*Breathe.  Receive.  Let it land.*

# Bridging the GAPS

When you take a step to acknowledge and move toward the call of your heart and soul, the Universe conspires to support you to receive it.

Watch for signs of support.  You might notice old doors closing.  New doors opening.  Burdens lifting.  People showing up in your life with helpful connections.  You feel gratitude for things you took for granted before.  Even the signs of nature appear differently.

Notice and acknowledge even the subtle signs.  Energy flows where attention goes.  Bridge the GAPS by focusing on Gratitudes, Affirmations and Positive Signs.  This will increase the flow of energy and open the space for more support of your intentions to flow into your life.  It will align and open you to receive your intentions into your life in a concrete way.

If you haven't noticed anything yet, ask for help from your guides.  There is much support available to you.  Be specific and relevant, and follow the flow to bridge the GAPS.

## GRATITUDES

_Today I am grateful for_ _____

_____

_____

_____

_____

_____

_____

_____

_____

# AFFIRMATIONS

# I am a Reflection of Divine Light.
# I am an Expression of Unconditional Love.
# I am a Manifestation of Divine Beauty.

Write & Recite the above affirmation
and/or add your own based on your intention:

_____

_____

_____

_____

_____

_____

_____

_____

_____

_____

_____

_____

# POSITIVE SIGNS

<u>Signs that the Universe supports my intentions are</u> _____

_____

_____

_____

_____

_____

_____

_____

_____

_____

_____

"Trying to resolve shame [or other feelings] that
does not belong to us is actually quite impossible.
One of the most powerful ways I work with clients
is to have them become aware of,
'Is this my shame or is this the other person's shame?'
The body clearly knows the difference."

~ Joan Brooks, from While We Were Silent

# Reflections & Ruminations

# Reflections & Ruminations

"What lies behind you and
what lies in front of you
pales in comparison to
what lies inside you."

~ Ralph Waldo Emerson

# 6: In Your Home

Now that you've taken an inventory and done a little house-cleaning, let's settle in and connect to your home - the body you live in.

Your body is a sacred temple, a wise living vessel that facilitates your journey on planet earth. It contains all of the light and insight of your spirit integrated with the wisdom and intelligence of the earth's elements.

Your body is designed to keep you safe and alive for this journey. It is an incredible mechanism that gives you messages from multiple vantage points to guide you on your journey.

Your physical sensations, gut feelings and instincts speak to you. Your experiences of movement, breath and sound give you guidance. Your sensory perceptions, your hearing, sight, touch, taste and smell - all of these are giving you information. Your thoughts, beliefs, opinions - all advising you. Your feelings, your emotions, the state of your life force - all messages.

At the most basic level, this information works together to keep you safe. At the core spirit level, they are guiding you home. These messages inform you about your relationship to your life experiences, your relationship with your deepest inner truths and your connection with your Highest Power.

During life's challenging events, there is a tendency to disconnect from the body and to lose trust in the body's messages. This is another way the body keeps you safe, and it's a natural part of the life journey.

The exercise in this chapter will help you connect with your body with love and compassion, to accept your body as your friend and partner on this journey to know your truth.

If anything does not feel safe for you, please skip it or modify it to suit your needs. Again, this is your journey. Make it work for you.

Your body is a Sacred Temple, the home of your Divine spirit. It is the spirit that gives breath to your lungs, rhythm to your heart and consciousness to your physical form. Without spirit, your body has no life.

Your body is masterfully designed to communicate to your consciousness everything it needs to know to navigate this journey and fulfill all the intentions you have come here to live into. It is the miracle that has brought you through your life challenges and to your healing path.

**#1:** Begin by calling on Your Source, Your Highest Power, whatever fits with your beliefs. I think of this as the Source of electricity that supplies the life force energy to my body. With the life force comes all the love, compassion, peace, light and capacity for forgiveness and gratitude. It is all that sources my ability to feel, to love, to live.

Call on your Source, and ask directly to be surrounded in Divine Light, Unconditional Love and Protection. Feel the energy surround you like a warm comforting blanket. You may need to use your imagination, or you may perceive in a different way. Trust. Everyone is different. Be true to you.

If you need help, ask your guides for help. You can also reach out to our community for support. (Find the info at BridgingTheGapsWorkbook.com)

*Recite aloud to hear your voice and reinforce safety for your mind and nervous system:*

## I am Light, I am Love, I am Safe. I am Home.

**#2:** Place your hands over your heart center, and breathe in the energy of Divine Light, Unconditional Love and Protection. Begin with easy gentle breaths. Focus your inhale directly into the space beneath your hands as if your heart is breathing in the stream of energy of Divine Light, Unconditional Love and Protection. If your heart feels guarded or closed, you can gently tap the heart center with your fingertips. As your heart relaxes, return to the breath.

*Repeat softly into your heart space:*

*I am Light, I am Love, I am Safe. I am Home.*

With each breath, allow your heart space to soften. Relax your shoulders, neck and jaw. If it feels okay for you, you can give a gentle massage to your jaw, neck and shoulders with gratitude.

**#3:** Stretch out your feet and toes, and circle your ankles. Feel your presence in your feet. Place your feet on the ground and feel your connection with the earth. Give gratitude to your feet for supporting you and carrying you.

Feel your energy moving into the earth - 3 feet, 5 feet, 7 feet, 10 feet beneath the earth's surface. Take a full gentle breath and allow yourself to sink into this connection. Breathe.

Now feel the energy of the earth supporting and nourishing you. Feel the energy coming up through your feet nourishing you with the wisdom of the earth elements and the grounding pulses of earth energy. Feel this wisdom infusing in with your energy and wisdom. Give gratitude to the earth for what it supplies to your body.

Breathe and rest into your home - your sacred temple.

*Recite:*

*I am Light, I am Love, I am Safe. I am Home.*

**#4:** Stretch out your arms to your sides. Circle your shoulders, arms and wrists and stretch out your fingers. Feel your presence into your hands and fingertips. Give gratitude to your hands for their service to you.

Rub your hands together and feel the energy between your hands. Move your hands apart slightly - can you still feel the energy between them?

Your hands are an extension of your heart. The Light, Love and Life Force energy of your spirit that moves through your heart also moves out through the palms of your hands. You may feel a focal point of energy right in the center of your palms where your heart energy reaches out through your hands.

Bring your right hand to your left shoulder and your left hand to your right shoulder. Allow the energy of your heart to gently hold and support you. Give yourself a heart hug.

*Repeat for yourself:*

### I am Light, I am Love, I am Safe. I am Home.

**#5:** If you are able, place the palm of your right hand on the sole of your left foot. Allow the energy that emanates from the center of your palm to connect with the energy at the center of the sole of your left foot. Hold this connection gently yet firmly as you focus on your breath.

*Repeat again:*

### I am Light, I am Love, I am Safe. I am Home.

Repeat this process with your left hand and right foot, or hold them both together.

### Breathe. Receive. Let it land.

# #6:
Shake out your hands.  Again, rub them together, allowing the energy between them to build.  Place your hands on your heart center, and focus on the Light, Love and Life Force energy that moves through your heart.  Feel the connection between your heart and your hands.

Now, as it feels comfortable for you, use the palms of your hands to gently pat your arms, moving from your shoulder down to your hand, first one side then the other.  You can give a gentle squeeze as you move down your arm if it feels okay for you.  Feel your presence in your arms and feel gratitude for their service.

*Repeat as you move through these steps:*

## I am Light, I am Love, I am Safe.  I am Home.

Next, use your palms to gently pat your legs, moving from your hips down to your feet, with a gentle squeeze making a safe, firm connection.  Feel your presence in your legs, and feel gratitude for their service.

You may want to stand and stretch your legs and hips.  You may find shaking or bouncing helpful as well.

*Repeat as you move through these steps:*

## I am Light, I am Love, I am Safe.  I am Home.

Next, gently tap or pat the top and sides of your head, your face, your jaw, neck, upper chest and shoulders.

Feel your presence in your head and face, your eyes, ears, nose and mouth.  Feel gratitude for their service.

*Repeat as you move through these steps:*

## I am Light, I am Love, I am Safe.  I am Home.

Next, gently tap or pat the back and sides of your torso.  If you can, cross over right hand to left side and left hand to right side.  Feel your presence in your core, and feel gratitude for its support and service.

*Repeat as you move through these steps:*

## I am Light, I am Love, I am Safe.  I am Home.

Next, if it feels safe for you, gently pat your belly.  You may want to rub your belly in a clockwise rotation.  This can be a tender space, and it houses many of your vital organs that do their best to keep you alive and healthy.  Allow your arms to cradle your belly as if holding a precious baby.  Send it love, acknowledgement and appreciation.

Feel your presence in your core, and feel gratitude for its service.

*Repeat again:*

## I am Light, I am Love, I am Safe.  I am Home.

**#7:**  Give gratitude to your Source for giving you this body and all its wisdom and strength.  You are a survivor, a bright light, a living spirit.  Everything you need to heal is inside you.

### Remember always:

## I am Light, I am Love, I am Safe.  I am Home.

"You think you are a small star,
when in fact you contain the whole Universe."

~ Sidi Shaykh Muhammad al-Jamal

# Creativity & Doodles

# Bridging the GAPS

When you take a step to acknowledge and move toward the call of your heart and soul, the Universe conspires to support you to receive it.

Watch for signs of support. You might notice old doors closing. New doors opening. Burdens lifting. People showing up in your life with helpful connections. You feel gratitude for things you took for granted before. Even the signs of nature appear differently.

Notice and acknowledge even the subtle signs. Energy flows where attention goes. Bridge the GAPS by focusing on Gratitudes, Affirmations and Positive Signs. This will increase the flow of energy and open the space for more support of your intentions to flow into your life. It will align and open you to receive your intentions into your life in a concrete way.

If you haven't noticed anything yet, ask for help from your guides. There is much support available to you. Be specific and relevant, and follow the flow to bridge the GAPS.

## GRATITUDES

_Today I am grateful for_ _____

_____

_____

_____

_____

_____

_____

_____

_____

# My body is a Sacred Temple that keeps me safe, grounded and connected to Earth.

Write & Recite the above affirmation
and/or add your own based on your intention:

_____

_____

_____

_____

_____

_____

_____

_____

_____

_____

_____

_____

# POSITIVE SIGNS

_Signs that the Universe supports my intentions are_ _____

_____

_____

_____

_____

_____

_____

_____

_____

_____

"We all process trauma similarly
because we have the same biology.
What we make of it moving forward
is what makes the difference."

~ Svava Brooks, from While We Were Silent

# Reflections & Ruminations

# Reflections & Ruminations

"Love is a fruit in season at all times,
and within reach of every hand."

~ Mother Teresa

# 7: What You Need

In order to safely and comfortably inhabit your home, you have basic human needs that must be met. In this chapter, we will look deeper into the Priorities you've identified earlier and discover what needs they are identifying for you.

PRIORITIES: Review your Priorities from Chapter 3. Which one feels most present for you right now? See the Example on the following page, and list your top priority on the worksheet that follows in section (1).

THOUGHTS: Usually when an issue is present for healing, the thoughts it invokes are closest to the surface. This includes the stories, reasons, rationalizations, the how's and why's, even the lessons and justifications. If these are present for you, identify your thoughts about this priority where indicated in section (2) of the worksheet.

FEELINGS: Identify the feelings underlying your thoughts. For this, you'll need to drop inside yourself and allow yourself to feel. This can be challenging because we've been taught it's not okay to feel. We've been conditioned to stuff our emotions and guard ourselves against feelings that might bring pain. Underneath your thoughts, what are you feeling?

Feelings are important to the healing process. They do not make you bad or weak or inferior. They give you vital information to discover and connect with your deepest inner truths. Give yourself permission to feel. Write your response in section (3).

Note: If you are using words such as "like, as if, if only, or because..." to describe your feelings, you are still in the thoughts. Take a deep breath and drop in deeper. What feelings belong to you. These are your feelings that no one can take from you or invalidate for you. You have a right to feel. Your feelings are important.

**The list of Feelings & Needs, tables 7.1 and 7.2, might give you clarity.

NEEDS: Beneath the feelings are needs. When you feel this way, what are you needing? Your feelings identify which basic needs you are missing. This is imperative to restoring yourself to wholeness. Review the list of Needs (7.2). These are needs that every human must have in order to feel safe in their bodies - the sacred temple. Write your response in section (4).

List your most relevant priority here:

(1) Priority #1 : _____Increase sense of self-worth_____

(2) Identify your thoughts about this priority:

I feel like other people are more deserving than me.  I put myself beneath other people, and my needs come last.  I feel unworthy   to ask for what I need.  I feel like other people perceive me as less than, somehow lower than them, simply insignificant.

(3) Now identify the feelings** underlying your thoughts:

Sadness, grief, despair, hurt, dejected

(4) Identify your needs** that this priority is informing for you:

Acceptance, compassion, (self-)forgiveness, love, nurturing, to be seen, to be known, to be understood, trust

** See list of Feelings and Needs Tables 7.1 and 7.2 for reference.

## 7: What You Need - Your turn...

List your most relevant priority here:

(1) Priority #1 : _____

(2) Identify your thoughts about this priority:

_____
_____
_____
_____

(3) Now identify the feelings** underlying your thoughts:

_____
_____
_____
_____

(4) Identify your needs** that this priority is informing for you:

_____
_____
_____
_____

** See list of Feelings and Needs Tables 7.1 and 7.2 for reference.

## OUR BASIC FEELINGS (table 7.1)

| | | | |
|---|---|---|---|
| Sadness | Fear | Dejected | Happiness / Joy |
| Grief | Anger | Self-Pity | Peace / Calm |
| Despair | Rage | Betrayed | Love |
| Hurt | Shame | Jealousy | Courageous |
| Disgust | Guilt | Envy | Confident |

## OUR BASIC NEEDS (table 7.2)

| CONNECTION | CONNECTION | PLAY | MEANING |
|---|---|---|---|
| acceptance | (cont'd) | joy | awareness |
| affection | support | humor | celebration of life |
| appreciation | to know and be | | challenge |
| belonging | known | HONESTY | clarity |
| cooperation | to see and be seen | authenticity | competence |
| communication | to understand and | integrity | consciousness |
| closeness | be understood | presence | contribution |
| community | trust | | creativity |
| companionship | warmth | PEACE | discovery |
| compassion | | beauty | efficacy |
| consideration | PHYSICAL | communion | effectiveness |
| consistency | WELL-BEING | ease | growth |
| empathy | air | equality | hope |
| inclusion | food | harmony | learning |
| intimacy | movement/exercise | inspiration | mourning |
| love | rest/sleep | order | participation |
| mutuality | sexual expression | | purpose |
| nurturing | safety | AUTONOMY | self-expression |
| respect/self-respect | shelter | choice | stimulation |
| safety | touch | freedom | to matter |
| security | water | independence | understanding |
| stability | | space | |
| | | spontaneity | |

Basic Needs from © 2005 by Center for Nonviolent Communication
Website: www.cnvc.org  Email: cnvc@cnvc.org  Phone: +1 505-244-4041

NOTE: Releasing the mental attachments to the stories of your life events can be challenging. The role of the mind is to be in service to the wisdom of your body and heart. It is not equipped to run the show. When you find yourself caught in racing thoughts or anxiousness, take a deep breath and ask yourself, "What am I feeling? What do I need?" Invite your mind to witness the responses of your body and heart. Allow the mind to shift into service of the needs and knowing of your heart.

## GUEST HOUSE

This being human is a guest house.

Every morning a new arrival.

A joy, a depression, a meanness,

some momentary awareness comes as an unexpected visitor.

Welcome and entertain them all!

Even if they're a crowd of sorrows

who violently sweep your house

empty of its furniture.

Still treat each guest honorably.

He may be clearing you out

for some new delight.

The dark thought, the shame, the malice,

meet them at the door laughing,

and invite them in.

Be grateful for whoever comes,

because each has been sent as a guide from beyond.

~ Jalal ad-Din Rumi

# Creativity & Doodles

# Bridging the GAPS

When you take a step to acknowledge and move toward the call of your heart and soul, the Universe conspires to support you to receive it.

Watch for signs of support. You might notice old doors closing. New doors opening. Burdens lifting. People showing up in your life with helpful connections. You feel gratitude for things you took for granted before. Even the signs of nature appear differently.

Notice and acknowledge even the subtle signs. Energy flows where attention goes. Bridge the GAPS by focusing on Gratitudes, Affirmations and Positive Signs. This will increase the flow of energy and open the space for more support of your intentions to flow into your life. It will align and open you to receive your intentions into your life in a concrete way.

If you haven't noticed anything yet, ask for help from your guides. There is much support available to you. Be specific and relevant, and follow the flow to bridge the GAPS.

## GRATITUDES

_Today I am grateful for_ _____

_____

_____

_____

_____

_____

_____

_____

_____

# My feelings give me valuable information that is vital to my life journey.

Write & Recite the above affirmation
and/or add your own based on your intention:

_____

_____

_____

_____

_____

_____

_____

_____

_____

_____

_____

# POSITIVE SIGNS

_Signs that the Universe supports my intentions are_ _____

_____

_____

_____

_____

_____

_____

_____

_____

_____

"To learn to accept ourselves in whatever state we are in,
To feel comfortable enough in ourselves to express who we are.
To know we can learn to provide care for ourselves
and ask for the help we need.
This is true FREEDOM."

~ Robyn McTague, from While We Were Silent

# Reflections & Ruminations

# Reflections & Ruminations

"We must let go of the life we have planned,
so as to accept the life
that is waiting for us."

~ Joseph Campbell

# 8: What You Know

Feelings inform you of what you need. What you need, you know.

A need is a feeling of separation from something - a missing of something vitally important. It indicates an inner knowing. If you did not have an experience and knowledge of something, how would you know you need it?

When I first moved to Florida, my neighbor had the most gorgeous mango tree I had ever seen. It was dripping with ripe, juicy mangos. I coveted those mangos. I craved those mangos.

If I did not have a knowledge - a firsthand experience - of the taste, texture, sweetness and juiciness of mangos, I would not have known to crave them.

The same is true for your Basic Human Needs. You came into this life with an encoded knowledge of your basic human needs. This knowing has stayed intact inside you no matter what has happened in your lifetime. This wisdom serves as an inner compass that guides you and directs you along your human journey.

This knowledge may be buried in your subconscious, but your subconscious is powerful, often more powerful than your conscious will.

Your experiences may have tainted your associations and beliefs of how to get those needs met or caused you to question whether you truly deserve to have those needs met. This is normal. You have probably recognized by now that your acquired habits are not getting you what you truly need.

When the old habits and belief patterns are no longer working for you, you experience dissatisfaction with a part of your life. The dissatisfaction is your wake-up call. It may show up as a discomfort or dissatisfaction or an illness or tragedy. It identifies the needs that are not being met. The needs lead you to the knowing that lies within.

The knowing is a bit stronger than the need. It feels more like a yearning - a yearning that guides you home to the center of yourself. It stems from your natural grief of separation from yourself, and it serves to guide you home to your core essence.

See the example on the following page. You can refer to a list of Yearnings in Table 8.1. Add your response to section (5) of the worksheet provided.

# 8: What You Know - example...

List your most relevant priority here:

(1) Priority #1 : ___ Increase sense of self-worth ___

(2) Identify your thoughts about this priority:

I feel like other people are more deserving than me. I put myself beneath other people, and my needs come last. I feel unworthy to ask for what I need. I feel like other people perceive me as less than, somehow lower than them, simply insignificant.

(3) Now identify the feelings** underlying your thoughts:

Sadness, grief, despair, hurt, dejected

(4) Identify your needs** that this priority is informing for you:

Acceptance, compassion, (self-)forgiveness, love, nurturing, to be seen, to be known, to be understood, trust

(5) Identify your Knowing - what you yearn for: **

I know the meaning of acceptance, compassion, forgiveness, love, connection, oneness. I know what it means to be seen, known, understood. to matter, to know trust and safety. This knowing is inside me, and I yearn to return to the knowing of my true Self.

** See list of Feelings and Needs on in Chapter 7, Tables 7.1 & 7.2, for reference. See the list of Knowings in Chapter 8, Table 8.1.

# 8: What You Know - Your turm...

List your most relevant priority here:

(1) Priority #_____ : _____

(2) Identify your thoughts about this priority:

_____

_____

_____

_____

(3) Now identify the feelings** underlying your thoughts:

_____

_____

(4) Identify your needs** that this priority is informing for you:

_____

_____

_____

(5) Identify your Knowing - what you yearn for:  **

_____

_____

_____

** See list of Feelings and Needs on in Chapter 7, Tables 7.1 & 7.2, for reference.  See the list of Knowings in Chapter 8, Table 8.1.

# YEARNINGS (table 8.1)

*Circle the Yearnings that you feel now and list them
on the previous page in section (5).*

Unconditional Love

Compassion

Acceptance

Trust

Forgiveness

Safety

Peace

Connection

Sovereignty

Strength

Patience

Friendship

Support

Cooperation

Self-Confidence

Belief & Trust in Self

To be valued

To be seen

To be heard

YEARNINGS (table 8.1)

To be understood

To be known

Purpose

Fulfillment

To know that I matter

To know that I'm not alone

To be ONE - Wholeness

...add your own...

"Know that you are not alone in your yearnings.
We all have them. Yours are yours.
Know them. Honor them. Voice them -
your innermost yearnings in your life."

~ Reggi Norton, M. Ac.

# Creativity & Doodles

# Bridging the GAPS

When you take a step to acknowledge and move toward the call of your heart and soul, the Universe conspires to support you to receive it.

Watch for signs of support. You might notice old doors closing. New doors opening. Burdens lifting. People showing up in your life with helpful connections. You feel gratitude for things you took for granted before. Even the signs of nature appear differently.

Notice and acknowledge even the subtle signs. Energy flows where attention goes. Bridge the GAPS by focusing on Gratitudes, Affirmations and Positive Signs. This will increase the flow of energy and open the space for more support of your intentions to flow into your life. It will align and open you to receive your intentions into your life in a concrete way.

If you haven't noticed anything yet, ask for help from your guides. There is much support available to you. Be specific and relevant, and follow the flow to bridge the GAPS.

## GRATITUDES

*Today I am grateful for* _____

_____

_____

_____

_____

_____

_____

_____

_____

# I am an eternal being.
# My yearning calls me home
# to my infinite existence.

Write & Recite the above affirmation
and/or add your own based on your intention:

_____

_____

_____

_____

_____

_____

_____

_____

_____

_____

_____

_____

# POSITIVE SIGNS

_Signs that the Universe supports my intentions are_ _____

_____

_____

_____

_____

_____

_____

_____

_____

_____

"I recognize that people struggle sometimes
in trying to find what their purpose is.
But don't ever stop searching,
don't ever stop asking the questions."

~ ALANI, from While We Were Silent

# Reflections & Ruminations

# Reflections & Ruminations

"The things that we love
tell us what we are."

~ Thomas Aquinas

# 9: Who You Are

The yearning for what you know inside yourself calls you home to your true essence. In reality, you have never been separate from yourself. This is only a perception, and it is a natural part of the course of life.

You are born with a knowing of your core essence, your Divine existence. That knowing stays intact inside you. It guides you throughout your life. It is the source of your higher knowing, your inner truth. It is a place inside you where you can experience inner peace and connection.

The experience of separation is a necessary illusion. In this life, we are given free will. In order to exercise free will, we have to forget our oneness with Unconditional Love. We experience the world of conditions and contrasts where there are distinctions between love and fear, right and wrong, good and bad, dark and light.

Once we have gained enough of what the contrasts are designed to teach us, we begin to awaken to the illusion of separation from love and we embark on the journey to return to the truth of oneness.

During the time of separation, we have a knowing of the truth - unconditional love and connection - but we are looking for it outside ourselves. We expect it from others and try to find contentment in material goods.

Once we realize that we cannot attain the unconditional love and connection from people or anything in the outside material world, we are left to turn inward and seek connection with a Higher Source.

This is the Divine design that guides us to a conscious knowing of the Divine existence within us. This is your journey to uncover and re-discover the Truth of who you are.

## KNOWING - I AM...

*Read and recite*

There is only Unconditional Love

I am accepted.  The Acceptance is within me.

I am forgiven.  The Forgiveness is within me.

I am safe.  The Safety is within me.

I am peaceful.  The Peace is within me.

I am seen.  The Seeing is within me.

I am heard.  The Hearing is within me.

I am understood.  The Understanding is within me.

I am known.  The Knowing is within me.

I am loved.  The Love is within me.

I matter.  The Meaning is within me.

I am connected.  The Connection is within me.

I am the sovereign caretaker of my domain.
The Sovereignty is within me.

The Life within me is the Breath of My Source.

I am connected with All That Is.


I AM ONE.

# KNOWING - I AM...

I yearn, therefore I know, therefore I am...
That which you yearn for is that which you know to be true.
The essence of your knowing is within you.

Which of the Knowings ring true for you?  What else would you add?
Reinforce your knowings by writing them in the space below.
*(Refer to your list of Yearnings in Chapter 8.)*

_____

_____

_____

_____

_____

_____

_____

_____

_____

_____

_____

_____

_____

_____

_____

_____

# Creativity & Doodles

# Bridging the GAPS

When you take a step to acknowledge and move toward the call of your heart and soul, the Universe conspires to support you to receive it.

Watch for signs of support. You might notice old doors closing. New doors opening. Burdens lifting. People showing up in your life with helpful connections. You feel gratitude for things you took for granted before. Even the signs of nature appear differently.

Notice and acknowledge even the subtle signs. Energy flows where attention goes. Bridge the GAPS by focusing on Gratitudes, Affirmations and Positive Signs. This will increase the flow of energy and open the space for more support of your intentions to flow into your life. It will align and open you to receive your intentions into your life in a concrete way.

If you haven't noticed anything yet, ask for help from your guides. There is much support available to you. Be specific and relevant, and follow the flow to bridge the GAPS.

## GRATITUDES

_Today I am grateful for_ _____

_____

_____

_____

_____

_____

_____

_____

_____

# My knowing leads me to my true sacred self.

Write & Recite the above affirmation
and/or add your own based on your intention:

_____

_____

_____

_____

_____

_____

_____

_____

_____

_____

_____

## POSITIVE SIGNS

_Signs that the Universe supports my intentions are_ _____

_____

_____

_____

_____

_____

_____

_____

_____

_____

"Who I am is not what I do,
but how I BE.
Self-love is my key to being."

~ Lilian Warman, from While We Were Silent

# Reflections & Ruminations

# Reflections & Ruminations

"Stop the words now.
Open the window in the center of your chest
and let the spirits fly in and out."

~ Jalal ad-Din Rumi

# 10: Transforming to YOU

Now it's time to close the gap between that which you know and the one who knows - between the knower and the known.

The true knowing is in the heart. Your true essence was breathed into you when you were in the womb. That pure light contains all the knowing of your Divine Essence. It is who you are. It has been in you all your life, but it has been covered over by the beliefs and perceptions you've acquired on your life journey. It has been hidden by the tricks your mind has played to keep you feeling safe.

In order to have true healing, which is true transformation, you must let go of the mind and allow the heart to carry you to your Truth.

Allow the breath between the Knower and that which is known at the depths of your heart to breathe together. Open your heart and allow it to carry you through the veils of the material realm to be one with your Divine Essence, the light of your existence.

This is the step of transformation. It is called the CAREFOR Connection - named for an acronym of its seven steps.

The steps are simple and equally profound. You are calling on your Source to enliven the Divine Essence within you, that which is who you are. You are calling it forth to resonate in your heart and to anchor in your core and in every cell of your body - to emanate through and from you, to BE YOU.

This requires openness and trust on your part and surrender to the wisdom of the All-Knowing. In order to find your true self, you must be willing to release attachments to all that you think you are and all that has brought you to where you are.

Read over the steps on the following page, then put them into practice for yourself. Let the yearning in your heart carry you. Be gentle and kind with yourself.

If you don't get it on the first try, keep trying. Some days my heart is more open than others. I have to keep trying or come back to it another time. In any case, take the opportunity to love yourself as you are.

When we call upon our Source, there is always some response. It may take time before we notice it, but trust that it is there.

Read through the following steps, then put them into practice. Follow these steps to Connect with the All-Knowing Source and allow your Knowing to transform your being into a conscious embodiment of who you are.

For each of the Knowings you listed in the previous chapter, repeat the following process:

**C**all upon your Source, your Highest Power. Call directly and imagine yourself sitting face-to-face, heart-to-heart with the Essence of your Source as your closest, most intimate and trusted mentor and friend.

**A**sk to receive the Knowing into your heart - for a direct energetic transmission of that which you yearn for to stream into the center of your heart.

**R**epeat the name of that Knowing into the center of your chest as you breathe it in. "Oh Divine _____." (insert knowings) For example, if you wrote "I am heard. The Hearing is within me," repeat, "Oh Divine Hearing."

NOTE: If you know the name of that Knowing in a Sacred Language, such as Arabic, Aramaic, Hebrew or Sanskrit, repeat the name in the Sacred Language.

**E**xtend your heart to energetically reach for the stream of energy that is dropping in - the vibration of the Knowing. Breathe it into yourself.

**F**ind the Sacred Jewel that is coming in for you through this transmission. You don't have to know it mentally. Observe and acknowledge what comes in whatever form it comes.

**O**pen your heart to allow the transmission - the gift or teaching that is being downloaded for you - to flow into your heart, fill your core and meet the essence within you.

**R**eceive with gratitude the healing transformation that is bringing you into conscious knowing and embodiment of your Sacred Essence and Oneness with the All That Is.

*Breathe. Receive. Let it land.*

# Bridging the GAPS

When you take a step to acknowledge and move toward the call of your heart and soul, the Universe conspires to support you to receive it.

Watch for signs of support.  You might notice old doors closing.  New doors opening.  Burdens lifting.  People showing up in your life with helpful connections.  You feel gratitude for things you took for granted before.  Even the signs of nature appear differently.

Notice and acknowledge even the subtle signs.  Energy flows where attention goes.  Bridge the GAPS by focusing on Gratitudes, Affirmations and Positive Signs.  This will increase the flow of energy and open the space for more support of your intentions to flow into your life.  It will align and open you to receive your intentions into your life in a concrete way.

If you haven't noticed anything yet, ask for help from your guides.  There is much support available to you.  Be specific and relevant, and follow the flow to bridge the GAPS.

## GRATITUDES

*Today I am grateful for* _____

_____

_____

_____

_____

_____

_____

_____

_____

# The All That Is transforms me into All That I Am.

Write & Recite the above affirmation
and/or add your own based on your intention:

_____

_____

_____

_____

_____

_____

_____

_____

_____

_____

_____

# POSITIVE SIGNS

_Signs that the Universe supports my intentions are_ _____

_____

_____

_____

_____

_____

_____

_____

_____

"At a distance,
you see only my light.
Come closer
and know that I am you."

~ Jalal ad-Din Rumi

# Reflections & Ruminations

# Reflections & Ruminations

"You are not a drop in the ocean,
You are the ocean
in a drop."

~ Jalal ad-Din Rumi

# 11: *Your Sacred Essence*

Every human being is a being of light - a reflection of Divine Light, an expression of Unconditional Love, and a manifestation of Divine Beauty.

AND - there is something extra special about the woman - an Essence so Sacred that many never even discover it in their lifetimes.

However, as a collective, it is our time.  Recent events in our culture are preparing us to evolve into a realm of the Sacred Feminine consciousness, and the healing of our humanity and our planet depends on our ability to embody this true Divine Nature.

Ironically, we have been templated with a lot of beliefs about women that are not true, and on a subconscious level - and perhaps even conscious - we're still programmed with many false beliefs.  We may be aligned with them or rebelling against them - either position is an acknowledgement that they hold some power over us and there is room for healing.

The key is to BE - to BE our Sacred Feminine Essence embodied and in harmony with our inner Sacred Masculine.

That's a tall order - a full course in itself.  For now, I want to share with you some key misbeliefs about women and the feminine, and help you to reframe your perspectives.

Our entire culture is built around the belief that men are superior in leadership, strength and mental capacity and therefore hold the responsibility to rule over the affairs of our nation - laws, businesses, finances, even moral decisions.

Our culture believes the woman is weak, emotional and cannot be trusted.  Much of these beliefs stem from our common interpretation (or misinterpretation) of the story of Adam and Eve - Eve was weak, gave into temptation and then seduced Adam into following her mistakes.  She doomed all humankind to a life of struggle and all women to be subservient to men.  It has even been written into our laws!

Our media portrays women as sex symbols, and the power of seduction is used to persuade - to set trends and influence billions of dollars in purchases.

From early ages, young girls and boys struggle to find an identity that fits with societal expectations and doesn't completely disregard the heart and soul. This leads us to make choices that gain the acceptance of others over being true to ourselves - a true struggle that lines the journey of every human being.

The dichotomy of the virgin or the whore - the wholesome clean-cut woman or the seductress - establishes the yo-yo effect between exploitation-and-shame and rigidity-and-constriction. Either extreme takes us off center and robs us of our deepest inner truths.

This whole construct is built on an illusion of separation. The good news is we can unplug from this illusion and drop into a reality that holds truths that honor the feminine in a Sacred Light for the powerful being she is designed to be.

One important distinction between women and men is the physical presence of the womb. The womb of the woman is a bridge between the worlds, an ocean of Divine Compassion. It is the bridge that brings forth life from Spirit into physical body. As women, we carry the energy of this pathway even if we have not given birth or if the womb has been removed.

There are many Divine secrets about this aspect of the woman. When we know the truth of it, the power it holds and the sacred passageway to the Divine Temple, we cannot disrespect it or allow it to be disrespected. We hold a doorway through which we can access and commune with Source - a doorway unique to the female body.

This is a very deep topic. For now, I offer you the following excerpt - a divine download included in the book, While We Were Silent. You are invited to read this aloud for yourself every night before you go to bed and every morning when you wake up. Keep it where you can see it and remind yourself of the truth of your Sacred Essence.

This is a deep healing for the body, mind, heart and spirit.

*NOTE: To find more information about the Sacred Feminine, the mystical and metaphysical meanings behind the Adam and Eve story, and more, visit BridgingTheGAPSworkbook.com.*

# MY SACRED ESSENCE

As a woman, I am created as a sacred being,

with gifts and abilities that are inherent in my creation,

that are extremely powerful,

beyond the power of this earthly realm.

I am worthy of love, honor and respect

- no less than that -

from anyone, including myself!

My divine essence is a bridge between the worlds,

a bridge to Source.

I carry the wisdom of earth and spirit.

I am a nurturer and protector of life,

a knower and connector of the subtle realms,

with true power and strength

beyond worldly physical strength.

This is a truth of creation,

a truth of existence,

and it does not change

regardless of what I have done or not done in my life.

This is not dependent on the beliefs I have in myself.

This is a Divine Truth.

*~ excerpt from While We Were Silent, Debra Graugnard*

# Creativity & Doodles

# Bridging the GAPS

When you take a step to acknowledge and move toward the call of your heart and soul, the Universe conspires to support you to receive it.

Watch for signs of support. You might notice old doors closing. New doors opening. Burdens lifting. People showing up in your life with helpful connections. You feel gratitude for things you took for granted before. Even the signs of nature appear differently.

Notice and acknowledge even the subtle signs. Energy flows where attention goes. Bridge the GAPS by focusing on Gratitudes, Affirmations and Positive Signs. This will increase the flow of energy and open the space for more support of your intentions to flow into your life. It will align and open you to receive your intentions into your life in a concrete way.

If you haven't noticed anything yet, ask for help from your guides. There is much support available to you. Be specific and relevant, and follow the flow to bridge the GAPS.

## GRATITUDES

_Today I am grateful for_ _____

_____

_____

_____

_____

_____

_____

_____

_____

# AFFIRMATIONS

## Write & Recite My Sacred Essence

Take 1-2 lines at a time.  Read aloud.  Read silently.  Write.  Breathe.

_____

_____

_____

_____

_____

_____

_____

_____

_____

_____

_____

_____

_____

_____

_____

_____

_____

_____

*Breathe.  Receive.  Let it land.*

# POSITIVE SIGNS

*Signs that the Universe supports my intentions are*

_____

_____

_____

_____

_____

_____

_____

_____

_____

*"We can't wait for someone else to make it okay
for us to be who we are meant to be.
We have to take the stance for ourselves,
with certainty,
and expect the outer world to organize itself
around our inner knowing. This is the way it works.
It begins with the inner and is then reflected on the outer."*

~ Debra Graugnard

# Reflections & Ruminations

# Reflections & Ruminations

"She remembered who she was
and the game changed."

~ Lalah Delia

# 12: Review & Reframe

I hope this journey has helped you to realize that what once may have felt like a shortcoming is in reality a doorway to uncover your true essence.

What called you to this pathway has birthed your intention.

Your commitment to yourself inspires your momentum to uncover the truth within you.

The path of self-exploration and discovery has guided you to your deepest inner knowing.

Your connection with the All That Is has transformed you to YOU.

You are a Sacred Being far more powerful than any force the material realm can possess.  You contain the knowledge and secrets of the universe within you.

You are an amazing being of light!

Let's lay out the specific pathway you've traveled and get a view of how far you've come.

We'll follow that with some reflection and examine how your perceptions have changed.

I'm truly excited for you and proud of you for making it through this process.  I'm excited for you to get a high-level overview and acknowledge just how far you've come.

If by chance it is not as far as you'd hoped, do not give up.  Keep going.  Seeds are planted long before we see their sprouts.

Transformation takes time, fortitude and courage. There is an infinite flow of grace supporting you in this process.  Celebrate and rejoice in being where you are now.

# 12: Review

Let's review the pathway you've traveled so far:

What called you here: (chapter 1) _____

_____

_____

Your intention: (chapter 1) _____

_____

_____

Your top priority(ies) (chapter 3) _____

_____

_____

What you have made space for: (chapter 4) _____

_____

_____

What you have discovered within yourself: (chapters 8)

*I know*_____

_____

_____

What truths have emerged from within you: (chapters 9)

*I am*_____

_____

_____

# 12: Reframe

How has your view of your priority or situation changed?

_____

_____

_____

_____

How has your view of yourself changed?

_____

_____

_____

_____

What does this mean for you now?

_____

_____

_____

_____

What does this mean for you moving forward?

_____

_____

_____

_____

# Creativity & Doodles

# Bridging the GAPS

When you take a step to acknowledge and move toward the call of your heart and soul, the Universe conspires to support you to receive it.

Watch for signs of support.  You might notice old doors closing.  New doors opening.  Burdens lifting.  People showing up in your life with helpful connections.  You feel gratitude for things you took for granted before.  Even the signs of nature appear differently.

Notice and acknowledge even the subtle signs.  Energy flows where attention goes.  Bridge the GAPS by focusing on Gratitudes, Affirmations and Positive Signs.  This will increase the flow of energy and open the space for more support of your intentions to flow into your life.  It will align and open you to receive your intentions into your life in a concrete way.

If you haven't noticed anything yet, ask for help from your guides.  There is much support available to you.  Be specific and relevant, and follow the flow to bridge the GAPS.

## GRATITUDES

_Today I am grateful for_ _____

_____

_____

_____

_____

_____

_____

_____

# In the perfection of the Divine Design,
# I am exactly where
# I'm supposed to be.
# I honor my TRUTH.

Write & Recite the above affirmation
and/or add your own based on your intention:

_____

_____

_____

_____

_____

_____

_____

_____

_____

_____

_____

# POSITIVE SIGNS

_Signs that the Universe supports my intentions are_

_____

_____

_____

_____

_____

_____

_____

_____

_____

_____

"Your task is not to seek for love,
but merely to seek and find all the barriers
within yourself that you have built against it."

~ Jalal ad-Din Rumi

# Reflections & Ruminations

# Reflections & Ruminations

"Gratitude unites
the material and the subtle worlds,
the heavens and the earths,
and makes the world into a
place filled with wonders."

~ Rosina-Fawzia al-Rawi

# 13: Gratitude

Gratitude is a powerful act. Of course, you know that. You've been practicing it throughout this workbook.

Gratitude aligns and opens you to the flow of gifts the Universe wants to bring through you. Gratitude also has many benefits for the body, mind, heart and spirit.

Physically, gratitude takes your nervous system out of Fight-Flight-Freeze mode and transitions you into the peaceful calming Rest-and-Digest mode. This releases stress in your body and prepares you to release the stuck energies of trauma.

Gratitude changes your subconscious programming. When you sincerely bow your heart in gratitude for what you have received, it opens your body-mind to more deeply receive the gifts and anchor the transformation into your cellular consciousness.

Using your voice and movement to express gratitude in a joyful way repatterns the old messages that have kept you bound in constriction, letting them know you are safe now.

Gratitude softens your heart and allows the light, love and compassion from within you to flow more freely. It transmits your sincere authentic expression to those around you.

Spiritually, gratitude brings you into connection with your Source. Gratitude brings you to recognize and witness the divine light and expression in everyone you meet and all natural life around you.

While we have noted specific gratitudes in each chapter, for this section note the gratitudes that pertain to your process you laid out in the Review & Reframe chapter.

Take time for celebration and rejoicing. Express your gratitude through writing, movement, art, song or vocal expression. You might also do something special for yourself or others. Do or be - whatever brings joy to your heart.

# Creativity & Doodles

# Bridging the GAPS

## GRATITUDES

Today I am grateful for _____

_____

_____

_____

_____

_____

_____

_____

_____

_____

_____

_____

_____

_____

_____

_____

_____

_____

_____

_____

_____

# I celebrate the truth
# of my sacred self.
# I am Light, Love, Beauty, Truth.

Write & Recite the above affirmation
and/or add your own based on your intention:

_____

_____

_____

_____

_____

_____

_____

_____

_____

_____

_____

## POSITIVE SIGNS

*Signs that the Universe supports my intentions are* _____

_____

_____

_____

_____

_____

_____

_____

_____

_____

_____

*"Your sensuality is your birthright.*
*It is what gives us so much pleasure and*
*brings us present in the moment,*
*feeling one's heartbeat or*
*enjoying the music or the birds or the ocean."*

*~ Donnalea Goelz, Ph.D., from While We Were Silent*

# Reflections & Ruminations

# Reflections & Ruminations

"We have what we seek,
it is there all the time,
and if we give it time,
it will make itself known to us ."

~ Thomas Merton

# 14: Setting Your Next Steps & Recommitting

Congratulations on completing this round of your journey! It's no small feat that you have stuck with the process and followed through with your commitment to yourself. I pray your journey has been an enlightening and transformational one.

Please do not underestimate your success. Take time to celebrate and integrate the changes into the core of your body. Give yourself a big heart hug! Take time for a warm Epsom salt bath with soothing or invigorating essential oils. Nourish yourself with a healthy meal enjoyed with a good friend.

Your journey is not over. In fact, it has just begun. As long as we are in human bodies, we're still traveling the path of self-discovery and transformation.

So where do you go from here?

In this chapter, we're going to look at your original priorities. In Chapter 3, you assessed the GAP between where you were and where you wanted to be for each priority you listed.

Now we're going to reassess. Has the gap narrowed? Has it broadened? Does that priority carry the same significance as it did in the beginning?

Then you'll look at what steps you want to take to continue your personal journey. How can you continue to anchor in what you've received? What do you want to put in place for yourself to continue your progress? What is next for you on your life pathway?

Note: If by chance you didn't realize what you had hoped for, this process is not meant for negative self-judgment. It is intended to give you information and create clarity.

Are you ready? Let's turn the page...

Priority #1: _____

*Your current state:*

On a scale of 1-5, with 1 being "I am looking for a way to get there" and 5 being "I'm there 100%," answer the following:

Where I want to be (A): _____ Where I am (B): _____ Gap: (A - B) _____

*Copy your original numbers from Chapter 3:*

Where I want to be (A): _____ Where I am (B): _____ Gap: (A - B) _____

Has the gap changed? By how much? _____

Has the significance of this priority changed? _____

_____

_____

Priority #2: _____

*Your current state:*

On a scale of 1-5, with 1 being "I am still searching for a way to get there" and 5 being "I'm there 100%," answer the following:

Where I want to be (A): _____ Where I am (B): _____ Gap: (A - B) _____

*Copy your original numbers from Chapter 3:*

Where I want to be (A): _____ Where I am (B): _____ Gap: (A - B) _____

Has the gap changed? By how much? _____

Has the significance of this priority changed? _____

_____

_____

# 14: Setting Your Next Steps

How can you continue to anchor in what you've received?

Some suggestions:
- Continue reflecting and writing your Gratitudes, Affirmations and Positive Signs.

- Journal your Reflections and Ruminations daily.

- Remember to celebrate your successes.

- Join or form a women's group to go through this process with you or join one of our online groups.. (Visit us at BridgingTheGapsWorkbook.com for suggestions.)

_____

_____

_____

_____

_____

What steps can you take to consciously continue your journey?
Do you need to repeat the process to continue to close the gap with an existing priority?  Is there a new priority you'd like to set for yourself?

My next Priority: _____

*This is important to me because*_____

_____

_____

On a scale of 1-5, with 1 being "I am still searching for a way to get there" and 5 being "I'm there 100%," answer the following:

Where I want to be (A): _____     Where I am (B): _____     Gap: (A - B) _____

# 14: Recommitting

To begin anew, take a moment and make a new commitment to yourself based on your next priority.

Date: _____

Dear _____,

_I commit to you_ _____

_____

_____

_____

_____

_____

_____

_____

_____

_____

_____

_____

_____

_____

_____

_____

_____

Your Signature -->            _____

_____

# Bridging the GAPS

When you take a step to acknowledge and move toward the call of your heart and soul, the Universe conspires to support you to receive it.

Watch for signs of support. You might notice old doors closing. New doors opening. Burdens lifting. People showing up in your life with helpful connections. You feel gratitude for things you took for granted before. Even the signs of nature appear differently.

Notice and acknowledge even the subtle signs. Energy flows where attention goes. Bridge the GAPS by focusing on Gratitudes, Affirmations and Positive Signs. This will increase the flow of energy and open the space for more support of your intentions to flow into your life. It will align and open you to receive your intentions into your life in a concrete way.

If you haven't noticed anything yet, ask for help from your guides. There is much support available to you. Be specific and relevant, and follow the flow to bridge the GAPS.

## GRATITUDES

_Today I am grateful for_ _____

_____

_____

_____

_____

_____

_____

_____

_____

# As I travel this life journey, every step takes me closer to subsistence in Divine Reality.

Write & Recite the above affirmation
and/or add your own based on your intention:

_____

_____

_____

_____

_____

_____

_____

_____

_____

_____

_____

_____

# POSITIVE SIGNS

_Signs that the Universe supports my intentions are_ _____

_____

_____

_____

_____

_____

_____

_____

_____

_____

_"As you live deeper in the heart,
the mirror gets clearer and clearer."_

~ Jalal ad-Din Rumi

# Reflections & Ruminations

# Reflections & Ruminations

# Creativity & Doodles

Thank you for sharing this pathway on our journey home.

We hope you'll continue to journey with us and
travel deeper into the center of your Self.

www.BridgingTheGAPSWorkbook.com

# Reflections & Ruminations

# Reflections & Ruminations

Creativity & Doodles

# Creativity & Doodles

"Each friend represents a world in us,
a world possibly not born until they arrive,
and it is only by this meeting that a new world is born."

~ Anaïs Nin

# Acknowledgements

I acknowledge with immense love and gratitude my Source, the Prophets, Saints, angels, guides, helpers, healers and all who have been a part of my life journey to teach me about the truth of who I am and to bring this work through for others.

I thank my spiritual teacher and guide, Sufi master and healer, Sidi Shaykh Muhammad al-Jamal for his patience and guidance and all that he gave to help me understand the inner landscapes and the expansive views and how they come together to reflect the Divine Reality through each of us and all that exists in this material realm. I thank my fellow travelers in the Shadhiliyya Sufi communities including teachers and students.

I thank all the authors and contributors to the While We Were Silent project: Lisa Hare, Dalzenia Sams, Dr. Anthousa Helena, Licia Berry, Carla Foster, Joan Brooks, Svava Brooks, Robyn McTague, Alani, Lilian Warman, Donnalea Goelz, Marta Luzim, Nkem Ndefo and Nancy Kern.

Gratitude for a special group of friends who formed the core beta group for this workbook, Reggi Norton, Rosemary Scavulo, Beth Allen, Aria Skye, Sandy Jo Norton and Jane Norby.

Gratitude to Fran Amendola Asaro and Tasha Chen who modeled how to use intentions, gratitudes and positive signs to manifest the desires of the heart.

I thank my partners at the former Illuminated Traveler group, Khadija and Noor Tyme Gigliotti, for all the hours of brainstorming and sharing of insights to hash out in plain English what is needed to find the way to the center.

A special thanks to all my clients and program participants over the years who have trusted me and at the same time taught me.

To all my biological family, thank you for sharing this journey called life, for the roles we've played to set the stage for each others' lesson plans and soul purposes, for your support and friendship, for teaching me about love.

Huge gratitude for all who will put this process into practice to let the inner light shine and make the world a brighter place.

# Thank You!

# References

PHOTOS:

Main cover photo: Two insects ladybirds on leaf curl spiral on a soft blurred green background. Adobe Stock Photo © Laura Pashkevich

Inset back cover photo: Ladybug with Spread Wings, Adobe Stock Photo © constantincornel

Pages 9 & 155, Africa Safari Animals Walking Down Path, Adobe Stock Photo © adogslifephoto

Page 67, Silhouette of Woman doing Yoga, Adobe Stock Photo © quickshooting

TABLES:

Table 7.2 Basic Needs from © 2005 by Center for Nonviolent Communication
Website: www.cnvc.org, Email: cnvc@cnvc.org, Phone: +1 505-244-4041

QUOTES SOURCES:

Good Reads, www.goodreads.com, 2019

Brainy Quotes, www.brainyquotes.com, 2019

Spirit Animal Totems, www.spirit-animals.com, 2019

Douglas-Klotz, Neil. (2005) *The Sufi Book of Life: 99 Pathways of the Heart for the Modern Dervish*. New York, NY: Penguin Group.

Pert, Ph.D., Candace B. (2010) *Molecules of Emotion.* New York, NY: Scribner Books.

al-Rawi, Rosina-Fawzia. (2015) *Divine Names: 99 Names of the One Love.* Northampton, MA: Olive Branch Press.

al-Jamal ar-Rifa'i as-Shaduli, Shaykh Muhammad. (2002) *Music of the Soul.* Petaluma, CA: Sidi Muhammad Press.

Graugnard, Debra et al, (2018) *While We Were Silent: 12 Experts Share Stories of Healing from Sexual Trauma.* USA: Totality Press.

# About Debra

Debra Graugnard, M.Div., is a best-selling Author, Speaker and an intuitive Spiritual Healing Practitioner with a Masters of Divinity in Spiritual Healing & Counseling,

Debra is a master healer and teacher in the Shadhiliyya Sufi Order. After 12 years working in the high-tech corporate environment, Debra experienced a spiritual awakening that changed her life forever. She was soon guided to a Sufi Master from Jerusalem, Sidi Shaykh Muhammad al-Jamal, who she studied with for 20 years, coming to know the inner workings of the Spirit-Heart-Body-Mind connection.

The steps outlined in this book are based on Debra's CAREFOR Connection Transformational Healing Process. Through this process Debra guides people to experience the Divine Essence within and to access and live their deepest Truths in everyday life.

Debra is also creator of the Community for Conscious Living and host of the Self-Care for the Soul podcast. She is especially passionate about helping people to realize how our daily habits and beliefs impact and influence all that exists in this beautiful planet so we can each make choices that create a sustainable environment and a peaceful world.

Debra facilitates transformative programs and retreats online and in-person. Learn more about Debra at www.JoyfullyLivingWellness.com.

# Connect with the Community & Learn More

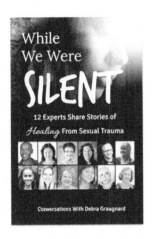

Visit JoyfullyLivingPublications.com to find other publications from Debra, including the Amazon #1 International Best-Seller, While We Were Silent: 12 Experts Share Stories of Healing from Sexual Trauma.

Women seeking healing from sexual trauma or seeking to understand and support others who have experienced sexual trauma, join our Private Facebook group: Facebook.com/groups/WhileWeWereSilent.

Visit JoyfullyLivingWellness.com to check out Self-Care for the Soul podcast, the Community for Conscious Living weekly Live Prayer & Healing Circle, Debra's blog and programs.

Visit BridgingTheGAPSWorkbook.com to access supplemental materials and group information for Bridging the GAPS workbook.

For general information or to contact Debra, visit
www.JoyfullyLivingWellness.com.